_____
To

_____
From

_____
Occasion

UNBRIDLED
Beauty

PAINTINGS BY
CHRIS CUMMINGS

HARVEST HOUSE PUBLISHERS

EUGENE, OREGON

UNBRIDLED *Beauty*

Published by Harvest House Publishers
Eugene, Oregon 97402
www.harvesthousepublishers.com

ISBN 978-0-7369-2487-0

Original artwork by Chris Cummings, Courtesy of Wild Wings, LLC,
Lake City, MN 55041, www.wildwings.com.

Design and production by Garborg Design Works, Savage, Minnesota

Contents

The essential joy of being with horses is that it brings us in contact with the rare elements of grace, beauty, spirit, and fire.

Sharon Ralls Lemon

FEARLESS AND *Fleet*

Imagine.

Wild horses—fearless and fleet. They gallop through the seasons in tune with a Power larger than they are. They heed signs almost unseen and know instinctively what the next step is.

The same is true of us. But we don't have to rely on mere instinct—we belong to the Creator of the universe, and our steps are never without purpose. In the wilderness of life, we have many paths to choose from. But we also have a faithful Companion to travel beside us on the journey. We may experience fear and anxiety about the unknown, second-guess our decisions, or struggle through pain, loss, and disappointment. But along the way we will see light through the shadows and experience lasting seasons of peace, joy, health, and prosperity.

Be at ease. Trust in the One who knows your destination. You will then be able to confidently walk, trot, or gallop through the adventures of life, fearless and fleet!

On the wings of the morning they gather and fly,

In the hush of the night time I hear them go by,

The horses of memory thundering through

With flashing white fetlocks all wet with the dew.

WILL H. OGILVIE
The Hooves of Horses

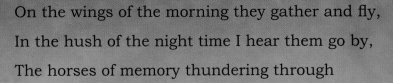

IN RIDING A HORSE WE BORROW FREEDOM.

HELEN THOMSON

"I know the plans
that I have for you,"
declares the Lord,
"plans to prosper
you and not to harm
you, to give you
hope and a future."

THE BOOK OF JEREMIAH

The mare set off for home with the speed of a swallow, and going as
smoothly and silently. I never had dreamed of such a motion, fluent
and graceful, and ambient, soft as the breeze flitting over the flowers,
but swift as the summer lightning.

RICHARD DODDRIDE BLACKMORE

Under his spurning feet, the road
Like an arrowly alpine river flowed
And the landscape sped away behind
Like an ocean flying before the wind.

THOMAS BUCHANAN READ

You have made known
to me the path of life;
you will fill me with
joy in your presence,
with eternal pleasures
at your right hand.

THE BOOK OF PSALMS

THE MERE SENSE OF LIVING
IS JOY ENOUGH.

EMILY DICKINSON

There's a whisper on the night wind, there's a star agleam to guide us, and the Wild is calling, calling, "Let us go."

AUTHOR UNKNOWN

FOR ONE TO FLY, ONE NEEDS

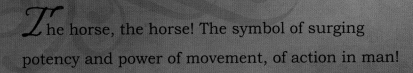

The horse, the horse! The symbol of surging potency and power of movement, of action in man!

APOCALPYSE

God created us with an overwhelming desire to soar…He designed us to be tremendously productive and "to mount up with wings like eagles," realistically dreaming of what He can do with our potential.

CAROL KENT

ONLY TO TAKE THE REINS.

MELISSA JAMES

In Step with the *Creator*

Wide open space. The possibilities seem endless. Horses embrace wild places with wide open hearts and unencumbered confidence. They alone hear some distant melody and respond in kind to the Musician. Suddenly, they may alter their course and sharply turn away from the path they were on. Only the Musician knows why—the horses do not need a reason. They have learned to recognize the sound of His still and gentle voice. Because He has proven Himself trustworthy, He calls and they respond. With joyful abandonment, they gallop to where He leads...to safety, to provisions of greener pastures, to fresher water, to solid footing.

We too must learn to respond to the melody that speaks to our hearts. God could be saving us from eminent unknown dangers or from harmful situations and relationships, or simply calling us to a richer life with Him. Whatever the call, we trust and obey the Voice we know and love.

He is pure air and fire; and the dull elements of earth and water never appear in him, but only in patient stillness while his rider mounts him. He is indeed a horse, and all other jades you may call beasts.

WILLIAM SHAKESPEARE
Henry V

God took a handful of southerly wind, blew his breath upon it, and created the horse.

BEDOUIN LEGEND

Since we live by the Spirit, let us keep in step with the Spirit.

THE BOOK OF GALATIANS

14

BE STILL, AND KNOW
THAT I AM GOD.

THE BOOK OF PSALMS

I can't tell you how much I long for you to enter this wide-open, spacious life. We didn't fence you in. The smallness you feel comes from within you. Your lives aren't small, but you're living them in a small way. I'm speaking as plainly as I can and with great affection. Open up your lives. Live openly and expansively!

THE BOOK OF 2 CORINTHIANS

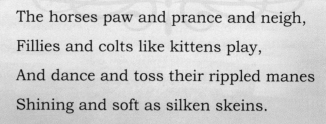

The horses paw and prance and neigh,
Fillies and colts like kittens play,
And dance and toss their rippled manes
Shining and soft as silken skeins.

OLIVER WENDELL HOLMES

To be loved by a horse, or by any animal, should fill us with awe—for we have not deserved it.

MARION GARRETTY

17

BUILT FOR *Relationships*

Even among wild horses a social structure, a sense of order, can be found. Horses care about and watch out for each other. The weakest members are often found in the safest spot—the middle of the herd, surrounded by loving and powerful members of the community. Those horses that "misbehave" are sometimes expelled from the herd. Isolation is truly a punishment for a creature built for companionship, but absolutely necessary for the benefit and smooth operation of the entire group. This social infrastructure allows each individual a safe haven in which to grow and thrive.

We are individually designed and endowed with a unique set of gifts and talents, but we are also built for relationships and a need for order. We have greater opportunities for discipleship when we feel secure enough to make new associations with others. A stable and orderly environment offers the freedom to develop healthy relationships with others and a genuine sense of community.

There is no secret so close as that between a rider and his horse.

ROBERT SMITH SURTEES

Horses can educate through firsthand, subjective, personal experiences, unlike human tutors, teachers, and professors can never do. Horses can build character, not merely urge one to improve on it. Horses forge the mind, the character, the emotions, and inner lives of humans. People can talk to one another about all these things and remain distanced and lonesome. In partnership with a horse, one is seldom lacking for thought, emotion, and inspiration. One is always attended by a great companion.

CHARLES DE KUNFFY

WE ARE BORN TO HAVE CONNECTION WITH GOD.

CLEMENT OF ALEXANDRIA

Just as our bodies have many parts and each part has a special function, so it is with Christ's body. We are many parts of one body, and we all belong to each other. In his grace, God has given us different gifts for doing certain things well.

THE BOOK OF ROMANS

Closeness, friendship, affection—keeping your own horse means all these things.

BERTRAND LECLAIR

No hour of life is wasted that is spent in the saddle.

WINSTON CHURCHILL

You took me to adventure and to love. We two have shared great joy and great sorrow. And now I stand at the gate of the paddock watching you run in an ecstasy of freedom, knowing you will return to stand quietly, loyally, beside me.

PAM BROWN

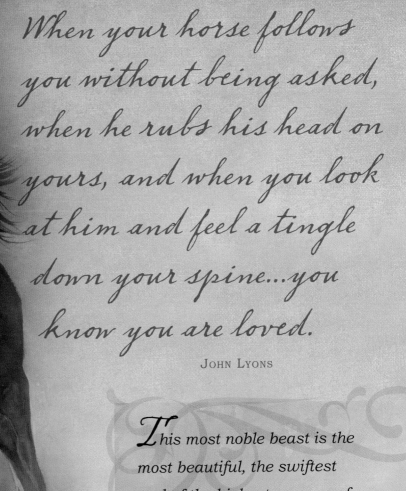

When your horse follows you without being asked, when he rubs his head on yours, and when you look at him and feel a tingle down your spine...you know you are loved.

JOHN LYONS

This most noble beast is the most beautiful, the swiftest and of the highest courage of domesticated animals. His long mane and tail adorn and beautify him. He is of a fiery temperament, but good tempered, obedient, docile and well mannered.

PEDRO GARCIA CONDE

REST AND
Refreshment

Wild horses know when to stop and drink. Running hard tests muscles to the fullest, and halting by a river to drink cool water will slake thirst, renew energy, and allow the herd to continue on, refreshed. It is just as vital to take time to rest as it is to perform to the fullest measure.

Running the race of life stretches us and often leaves us with parched hearts and tired bodies. These are the times to stop by the river—when we are tired and in need of refreshment. When there are miles to go, yet we are weary. Come. Drink. Quench your thirst in the stream of living water.

*T*hrough the days of love and celebration and joy, and through the dark days of mourning—the faithful horse has been with us always.

ELIZABETH COTTON

A generous man will prosper; he who refreshes others will himself be refreshed.

THE BOOK OF PROVERBS

LET MY SOUL TAKE REFUGE...
BENEATH THE SHADOW OF
YOUR WINGS: LET MY HEART,
THIS SEA OF RESTLESS WAVES,
FIND PEACE IN YOU, O GOD.

AUGUSTINE

*T*he day is done,

The sun has set,

Yet light still tints the sky;

My heart stands still

In reverence,

For God is passing by.

RUTH ALLA WAGER

May He support us all the day long, till the shades lengthen, and the evening comes, and the busy world is hushed, and the fever of life is over, and our work is done! Then in His mercy may He give us a safe lodging, and a holy rest, and peace at the last.

JOHN HENRY NEWMAN

Reliable friends who do what they say are like cool drinks in sweltering heat—refreshing!

THE BOOK OF PROVERBS

Whoever is thirsty, let him come; and whoever wishes, let him take the free gift of the water of life.

THE BOOK OF REVELATION

HORSES CAN'T TALK,
BUT THEY CAN SPEAK
IF YOU LISTEN.

AUTHOR UNKNOWN

A horse loves freedom, and the weariest old work horse will roll on the ground or break into a lumbering gallop when he is turned loose into the open.

GERALD RAFERTY

TO ME, HORSES AND FREEDOM ARE SYNONYMOUS.

VERYL GOODNIGHT

*O*ne who loves is borne on wings; he runs, and is filled with joy; he is free and unrestricted. He gives all to receive all, and he has all in all; for beyond all things he rests in the one highest thing, from whom streams all that is good.

THOMAS À KEMPIS

Grace unto you, and peace, be multiplied.

THE BOOK OF 1 PETER

GENTLE
Strength

So often when we think of horses
we think of their physical power, but their sense of smell is one
of the strongest resources horses use to navigate their everyday
lives. Odors carried on a breeze can be used to advantage in the
herd. A mare uses smell to pick out her foal from others or to
locate the nature and direction of danger. The lead horse uses
smell to direct the herd to shelter in advance of a storm or to
water in the dry heat of summer. Although the wind is unseen,
horses are attuned to it and use it to their advantage.

A gentle breeze flows through our lives as well. It surrounds
us, directing us to shelter or giving us strength just when we
need it. When we quiet ourselves, we will sense the presence of
something graceful in form and of unseen strength. It is a warm
zephyr, blown from heaven itself. A sacred, holy wind.

$\mathcal{G}$od's strong hand is on you; he'll promote you at the right time. Live carefree before God; he is most careful with you.

THE BOOK OF 1 PETER

The horse, with beauty unsurpassed, strength immeasurable and grace unlike any other, still remains humble enough to carry a man upon his back.

AMBER SENTI

Be beautiful inside, in your hearts, with the lasting charm of a gentle and quiet spirit which is so precious to God.

THE BOOK OF 1 PETER

In the forest we can learn life's lessons if we will—

How to turn towards the sunshine, standing straight and still,

How to be content with slow development and grow

In grace and strength in spite of storms, of wind and frost and snow.

PATIENCE STRONG

The wind of heaven is that which
blows between a horse's ears.

ARABIAN PROVERB

Ah, steeds, steeds, what
steeds! Has the whirlwind a
home in your manes? Is there
a sensitive ear, alert as a flame,
in your every fiber? Hearing the
familiar song from above, all
in one accord you strain your
bronze chests and, hooves barely
touching the ground, turn into
straight lines cleaving the air, and
all inspired by God it rushes on!

NIKOLAI V. GOGOL

Those who hope in the Lord
will renew their strength.
They will soar on wings
like eagles; they will run
and not grow weary, they
will walk and not be faint.

THE BOOK OF ISAIAH

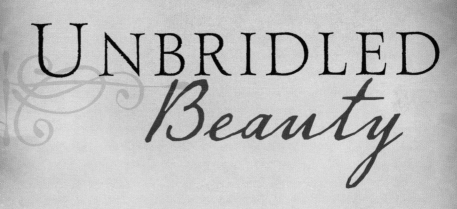

UNBRIDLED
Beauty

A horse under bridle is controlled and unable to go where he pleases. Though noble creatures, horses can easily become timid when restrained. Horses in the wild, however, are free to explore, boldly roaming at will throughout the landscape, showing no fear, splendid in their movements.

We also long to be unbridled. We can step out from under the constraints that come against us when we free God from the box we've placed Him in, and then the great adventure can begin. We can grow spiritually and emotionally. "Where the spirit of the Lord is, there is freedom"—freedom to decide for ourselves what to say yes to, what to say no to. Freedom to travel the wild, unspoiled paths, the high passes where only God can lead. Let the journey begin!

God who is goodness and truth is also beauty. It is this innate human and divine longing, found in the company of goodness and truth, that is able to recognize and leap up at beauty and rejoice and know that all is beautiful, that there is not one speck of beauty under the sun that does not mirror back the beauty of God.

ROBERTA BONDI

I am still under
the impression
that there is
nothing alive
quite so beautiful
as a horse.

JOHN GALSWORTHY

GOD IS SHEER BEAUTY,
ALL-GENEROUS IN LOVE,
LOYAL ALWAYS AND EVER.

THE BOOK OF PSALMS

A lovely horse is always an experience.
It is an emotional experience of the
kind that is spoiled by words.

BERYL MARKHAM

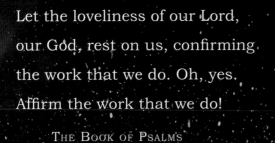

Let the loveliness of our Lord,
our God, rest on us, confirming
the work that we do. Oh, yes.
Affirm the work that we do!

THE BOOK OF PSALMS

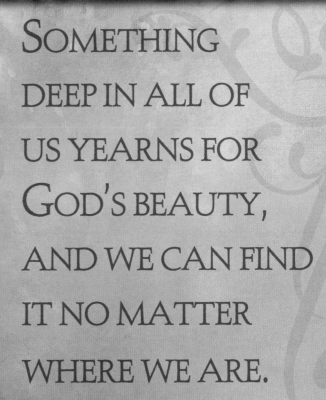

SOMETHING
DEEP IN ALL OF
US YEARNS FOR
GOD'S BEAUTY,
AND WE CAN FIND
IT NO MATTER
WHERE WE ARE.

SUE MONK KIDD

Life is so full of meaning and
purpose, so full of beauty, beneath
its covering, that you will find that
earth but cloaks your heaven.

FRA GIOVANNI

The sight of him did something to me I've never quite been able to explain. He was more than tremendous strength and speed and beauty of motion. He set me dreaming.

WALT MOREY

The most beautiful, the most spirited and the most inspiring creature ever to print foot on the grasses of America.

J. FRANK DOBIE

*God hasn't invited us into a disorderly,
unkempt life but into something holy and beautiful—
as beautiful on the inside as the outside.*

THE BOOK OF 1 THESSALONIANS

BEAUTY IS NOT CAUSED. IT IS.

EMILY DICKINSON

Horses—if God made anything more beautiful, He kept it for Himself.

AUTHOR UNKNOWN